TO:

_____

FROM:

_____

PRACTICING
the PRESENCE
of JESUS

Wally Armstrong

Summerside Press™
Minneapolis, MN 55378
www.summersidepress.com

Practicing the Presence of Jesus

© 2012 by Wally Armstrong
ISBN 978-1-60936-702-2

Unless otherwise noted, Scripture references are taken from The New American Standard Bible® (NASB), copyright © 1960, 1962, 1963, 1968, 1971, 1972, 1973, 1975, 1977, 1995 by The Lockman Foundation. Used by permission. Other Scripture references are taken from the following sources: The Holy Bible, New International Version®, NIV®, Copyright © 1973, 1978, 1984, 2011 by Biblica, Inc.™ Used by permission of Zondervan. All rights reserved worldwide. *The Message.* Copyright © 1993, 1994, 1995, 1996, 2000, 2001, 2002 by Eugene Peterson. Used by permission of NavPress, Colorado Springs, CO. All rights reserved.

Stock or custom editions of Summerside Press titles may be purchased in bulk for educational, business, ministry, fundraising, or sales promotional use. For information, please e-mail specialmarkets@summersidepress.com.

Cover and interior design by Thinkpen Design, Inc. | www.thinkpendesign.com

Summerside Press is an inspirational publisher offering fresh, irresistible books to uplift the heart and engage the mind.

Printed in China

To my Savior, Lord, Friend, and Companion—Jesus.

To the Father and the Son be all honor
and glory forever and ever.

"We all hunger for connection, for friendship, and for more in this life. Wally Armstrong has written a powerful book that will help you find what your heart longs for most."

—KEVIN G. HARNEY, PASTOR AND AUTHOR OF *RECKLESS FAITH*

"When I first met Wally and learned his story of coming to know Jesus in the profoundly personal way he describes in this book, I was incredibly heartened and amazed. Here was someone who had discovered the beauty of imaginative prayer and begun to be transformed by Jesus in the same way I had about ten years ago! This book is written by a man who loves Jesus, is loved by Jesus, and who wants you to discover that same kind of love relationship with Jesus too."

—CHRISTIANNE SQUIRES, WRITER AT WWW.STILLFORMING.COM

"Wally's book will have a profound impact in our 'church' culture, where we have been raised up in the faith with sacraments and doctrine. We get the 'performance' aspect of faith, but we long for the experience."

—BILL BOHLINE, PASTOR, HOSANNA! CHURCH

"Wally's transparency and quest regarding his desire to experience Jesus' presence in everyday life is something we can all identify with. This book will inspire you to know Jesus not just as a Savior but as a close friend and companion."

—CRAIG ALTMAN, PASTOR, GRACE FAMILY CHURCH

Speaking as a pastor for over thirty years, I can testify how easy it is to be more like Martha (busy serving in Jesus' name) and not enough like Mary (experiencing Jesus himself). After hearing and reading Wally's story and testing out the "chair experiment" on myself and others, I can confirm that practicing the presence reawakened my spirit, soul, and body to his reality and friendship."

—MATTHEW NAIL, PASTOR, THE CHURCH AT QUAIL CREEK

"This book brings into focus an important but often neglected aspect of our Christian faith—our personal relationship with God through his Son Jesus. With a refreshingly new look at that relationship, Wally helps us 'see God' and, in doing so, assists us in deepening our faith and experiencing Jesus in a remarkable new way."

—DR. RICK ALEXANDER, PHYSICIAN

"This is my commandment, that you love one another, just as I have loved you. Greater love has no one than this, that one lay down his life for his friends. You are My friends if you do what I command you. No longer do I call you slaves, for the slave does not know what his master is doing; but I have called you friends, for all things that I have heard from My Father I have made known to you."

—JOHN 15:12–15

Thanks be to Thee, my Lord Jesus Christ,
   for all the benefits Thou hast given me,
   for all the pains and insults
   which Thou hast borne for me.
O most merciful Redeemer, Friend, and Brother,
   may I know Thee more clearly,
   love Thee more dearly,
   follow Thee more nearly,
   day by day.
Amen.

—ST. RICHARD OF CHICHESTER

contents

Foreword

WALLY AND I ARE IN MANY WAYS SOUL MATES. We share two loves: the love of golf and the love of Jesus.

I began golfing at the age of six and have loved the game ever since. That was why it was such a joy for me to coauthor *The Mulligan* with Wally.

My love of Jesus came much later. In fact, I was in my late forties when I began to read Matthew, Mark, Luke, John, and Acts—and realized that everything I had ever written or taught about leadership, Jesus had done, perfectly, with his twelve inexperienced followers. In fact, he was the greatest leadership role model of all time.

Wally shares my belief about Jesus being the greatest leadership role model of all time, but he insists that I use the word *is* rather than *was*. Why does he insist on that emphasis? Because Wally believes that Jesus is here today to guide not only our leadership but also our life journey. He is convinced that Jesus is our friend and is available to us every day, if we will only take the time to invite him into our lives.

Read this book and soak in Wally's story. I guarantee you will develop a clear way to meet Jesus face-to-face every day and experience his transforming friendship.

—KEN BLANCHARD, COAUTHOR OF *THE ONE MINUTE MANAGER*® AND *LEAD LIKE JESUS*

preface

RECEIVING JESUS CHRIST AS YOUR PERSONAL LORD AND SAVIOR is the most important event in any and every life. It is the centerpiece of the Christian faith. Yet there's an overlooked gift that was powerfully exercised by the early followers of Jesus that has been laid aside by modern Christianity. That gift is receiving the offer from Jesus to become his friend, and that's what this book is all about.

I have found that there are countless believers who are striving to live a life of faith, just like I did for many years, and who are trying so hard to become like Jesus in their own strength. It is exhausting! But the amazing truth is that Jesus is standing right beside each one of us, offering us the life-changing gift of his friendship and the promise of transformation from the inside out. The reality of the believer's life should not be about our own efforts to become disciples of Christ. It is about learning to experience Jesus as real and practicing his presence in our daily lives. It is about moving from "I am a believer in Jesus" to "I am a follower of Jesus." This is how true transformation happens.

The common denominator of all Christian denominations, all twenty-eight thousand of them, is that Jesus is risen and is still alive. And if he is still alive, then he is here today and is as real as he was two thousand years ago. I confess that I knew this in my mind for nearly forty years, but the implications of what this meant never really occurred to me until I had the experience that I will share with you in this book.

If you haven't experienced the transforming friendship of Jesus, it is my hope that you will receive this wonderful gift. It's really nothing new, for Jesus has been offering it since the very moment he stepped onto the shores of Galilee and called a rugged fisherman named Peter to follow him and be his friend. He still calls to us with that same invitation, and he will come to you—if only you will accept the gift of his presence.

1

seeing jesus at the masters

"THE GUY TALKING TO BEN CRENSHAW? OH, THAT'S JESUS."

I did a double take.

There was Ben Crenshaw, the former Masters champion, at the center of the crowd, and the fellow talking with him was a tall, handsome golfer who was wearing the "uniform": khaki pants and a golf shirt with the Masters logo. I must have looked at least a little puzzled because my friend added, "You know, Jim Caviezel—the guy who played Jesus in *The Passion of the Christ*."

My friend, Jim Hiskey, told me Caviezel was at the Masters to promote his upcoming movie *Bobby Jones: Stroke of Genius*, in which he was playing the title character and golfing legend. Bobby Jones was the designer, in fact, of the very golf course on which we were standing. I hadn't seen *The Passion of the Christ* movie yet, which accounted for my difficulty in recognizing the actor, but my friend's granddaughter said Caviezel had been generating quite a bit of interest during the week.

I tucked away the image of my friend Ben Crenshaw having a friendly chat with "Jesus," not realizing at the time the significance of that moment. Only later that evening would the memory of it take on a deeper meaning—compelling, among other things, the writing of this book.

That week in the spring of 2004, I had driven up to Augusta, Georgia, from my home in Florida to follow the great Arnold Palmer. It would likely be his final outing in the tradition-rich Masters, possibly the most legendary tournament in the golfing world. I'm a longtime recruit in "Arnie's Army"—it would be hard for me to count up all the great memories I have of watching Arnold Palmer charge the course in the closing holes of a tournament. He'd hitch up his pants and lash away at the ball with that quick, low swing of his, inventing impossible shots and sinking putts that anybody else would have been glad to leave within three feet of the cup. Even though I went on to play in over three hundred PGA Tour events myself, including several Masters, I never got over my admiration for Arnie.

I had arrived in time to join his gallery on about the fourth or fifth hole, where the Augusta National was proving a bit too arduous for the aging Arnold Palmer. Still, even though he wasn't likely to be in serious contention for the final rounds, I couldn't imagine anything I wanted to do more than follow my hero on his final tour of this course. It was here that he had generated so many thrilling moments during his career.

During Arnie's round, I bumped into my good friend Jim Hiskey, and we walked a few holes together. Jim told me he had to meet up with his granddaughter, Rachel, behind the eighteenth green and asked me to come up to meet them in an hour or so. When I arrived to meet them behind the green, that's when I noticed the crowd of people off to the side. I stepped closer to investigate...and the rest you know.

That evening, on my way to spend the night at the home of some friends, I pulled into a local convenience store parking lot to conduct a telephone interview I had scheduled with the syndicated radio show for *Sports Spectrum* magazine. I'm on the show fairly frequently, especially in the days leading up to major tournaments, and the interviewer asked me most of the usual questions: what kind of shape the course was in, what were my thoughts on who'd be in contention that year, and what was it like following Arnie on what would likely be his last appearance at Augusta.

Then I recall the interviewer saying, "Okay, Wally. We've got about thirty seconds left. Anything else you'd like to tell our listeners before we run out of time?"

Without thinking, I said the first thing that popped into my head. "Oh, yeah! Today I came around behind the eighteenth green and saw Jesus talking to Ben Crenshaw!"

> That day, "Jesus" looked like one of us...and that was exactly the point.

There was a moment of stunned silence. They call it "dead air" in the broadcasting business. Then the interviewer recovered. "You...saw who?"

"The actor—the guy who played Jesus in *The Passion of the Christ*," I said, trying to redeem myself. But it was too late. I heard a *click* and the line was dead. The interview was over. I snapped my cell phone shut. *Nice one, Wally*, I thought. *They probably think you are some kind of nutcase.*

But almost as soon as I snapped my phone shut, the strong impression came into my mind that there was something really right about what I'd said. In fact, that glimpse of "Jesus" on the golfing green provided a crowning of sorts on what had become one of the most important spiritual discoveries of my life—a truly transforming experience that made the presence of Christ so real and brought me into a deeper, more meaningful relationship with him than I had ever dreamed possible.

Standing in the midst of the crowd talking to Ben Crenshaw, Jim Caviezel had looked like any of hundreds of men at Augusta that day. He wore no robe, no sandals, and no beard—nothing like the images many of us remember from Sunday school when someone refers to Jesus. That day, "Jesus" looked like one of us…and that was exactly the point.

All of this was running through my mind that evening as I concluded my interview. My "spiritual outburst" might have made me sound like a nutcase to some. But I also realized that there was a sense in which my experience earlier that day at Augusta was a very fitting symbol for a pilgrimage I had been taking the past four and a half months. It was drawing me deeper into the most important friendship of my life.

You see, a few months before, I was motivated by a deep spiritual hunger. That was the impetus to embark on an experiment of sorts. Even though I had been a committed follower of Christ for most of my adult life, I felt continually frustrated by my inability to get a really firm grip on just who Jesus is and how to relate to him. I had accepted Jesus as my Savior and Lord thirty-six years before, and there was no doubt in my mind that my eternal destiny was secure. But despite that and many opportunities to share Christ with thousands of others around the world, I still sensed I was missing something.

I am a businessman—a professional golfer, actually—and my profession is the most performance-driven career in the world. Unlike other professional athletes, golfers get no six-figure, five-year contracts—or any guarantees at all starting each year. Our success is measured solely by the money we make, and the "money list" is published for everyone to see. What's more, I had to finish in the top sixty on the money list or I would lose my playing privileges. It doesn't matter how well you play, what your track record has been over the long haul, or what your potential for the future might be. Losing your card means you have to go back to the grueling qualifying school and compete with over two thousand other aspiring pros who are all shooting for twenty-five one-year cards. Now that's pressure!

> I applied the same discipline
> to my faith walk as I had to golf.

When I accepted Jesus into my life in the late 1960s, I brought that same performance-driven mentality into my relationship with him. I worked as hard as I could to gain his approval. I read all the current books on how to live the Christian life, and I applied the same discipline to my faith walk as I had to golf.

Now, don't mistake me. God can use even a type-A overachiever like me to accomplish his will. Nor is there any question in my mind that I was saved. If receiving God's gift of grace is dependent upon our perfectly understanding and living out its implications, none of us has any hope whatsoever. But remember what Jesus said? "Come to me, all you who are weary and burdened, and I will give you rest.... My yoke is easy and my burden is light" (Matthew 11:28, 30 NIV). He also said, "I have come that they may have life, and have it to the full" (John 10:10 NIV). I hadn't yet found that rest or light burden or full life Jesus talked about.

In fact, I was so busy doing things for Jesus that I hardly had any time left over to just be with him. And for a long time, I didn't know any better. I thought that was the way it was supposed to be. The truly good news is, indeed, "Jesus paid it all," but the way I was living, my version would have run something like, "and now you get to pay him back."

The thing is, when I worked hard at practicing my faith, I felt good about my relationship with Jesus. But when I slacked off, I felt like a failure. It was an on-again, off-again relationship, and I was so frustrated by it. When I tried to communicate with Jesus, it felt awkward and I felt guilty. I had no clear picture of him in my mind—just a fuzzy image based on childhood experiences and second-hand information.

Now, you might think that a guy who had spent most of his adult life playing a game he loves and talking to people about a Savior he loves couldn't possibly want anything. What reason could I have to feel such spiritual distraction? Still, I did feel it, and I was quickly running out of ideas about how to escape it.

But all of that changed in an instant the day I encountered an invitation that turned everything upside down—or rather, right side up.

2

SOLD OUT AND WORN OUT

DO YOU REMEMBER THE SCENE IN *NATIONAL TREASURE* when Nicolas Cage's character is standing in the room about a jillion feet beneath Trinity Church in Manhattan, staring at the notch in the wall? He'd been on a search for a vast, unimaginable treasure that was hidden by a centuries-old secret society. It was the wealth of the ages, guarded by secrecy from public knowledge. It was also the obsession not only of Cage's character, but also that of his father, his grandfather, and generations of his family before him.

In that scene, he looks down at the object in his hand and realizes that its shape matches exactly the notch in the wall. It is the key to whatever is on the other side of the secret door. To get to this moment, he has traveled the frozen wastelands of the Arctic Circle and dodged bullets on city streets. He has been mocked, threatened, sought by law enforcement agencies, and nearly killed. Realizing that he is about to either solve the biggest mystery of all time or encounter another dead end, he says, almost in a whisper, "Can it really be that simple?"

> The book talked about entering into a relationship with Jesus in the here and now—as if he were a person in our modern world.

That's kind of how I felt on that day, four months before I saw "Jesus" on the eighteenth green in Augusta. I was opening a package I had just received from a mail-order bookstore in Wisconsin. I removed the contents: a used copy of a little red leather-bound book first published in London in 1929. The book's title was *The Transforming Friendship: The Reality of the Presence of Jesus Among People Like Ourselves*. The advertisement had said the book talked about entering into a relationship with Jesus in the here and now—as if he were a person in our modern world.

Like Nicolas Cage's character in *National Treasure*, I had been on a restless quest for a great treasure. Also like him, I had run up against my share of blind alleys. Though I had been a follower of Christ for almost forty years, I had never felt that I "got it." Somehow the knowledge of the presence of Christ wasn't as real and precious to me as Scripture seemed to promise it would be. Still, the relentless desire to know and to understand what was really at the core of the life of faith had been driving me ever since that day in 1968 at the University of Florida when I gave my life to Christ.

So how is it possible for a guy to be a committed believer in Christ like I was for so many years and still miss out on the friendship offered to him by Jesus? For me, the explanation goes back to my desperate need to succeed, a need that began as a young boy in Indiana. We lived in America's heartland, but my boyhood didn't look much like *Leave It to Beaver*, or anything else on TV in those days.

My dad came back from World War II, and, like many of the guys from the Greatest Generation, he had to find a job. He had a background and great interest in music and the arts, but during the postwar boom, sales offered a better way to feed a growing family. So my dad became a road warrior—gone Monday through Friday, calling on customers all over the state, then coming home on the weekends. In later years, I would come to understand a little bit of his resentment at never having a chance to pursue his dreams. As Dad put it, he never got the breaks.

Over the years, to stick a bandage on his inner hurts, he started drinking. He spent much of his weekends at home in some stage of intoxication. Unfortunately, liquor didn't mellow out Dad; it just made him meaner.

I was the oldest of three boys, so during the week I was pretty much the man of the house, as far as my mom and brothers were concerned. That also meant that on the weekends, when Dad was home, I became the focal point for his resentment over his lot in life. I grew up feeling that nothing I did suited him. I just couldn't measure up. I was lazy or dumb or too slow bringing in the newspaper or whatever. There was never any physical abuse, but his words cut me like a whip. He was verbally abusive of me, my mom, and my brothers.

I remember well the hot shame of his accusations aimed at my mother, though they came right through the knotty pine walls of my bedroom and into me. *Why is Wally so messed up? Why can't he do anything right? How come nobody around here is on my team?* And on and on, like a broken record.

My mom would try to defend me, but Dad would just crank up the volume. A few times, it got so loud that my brothers and I would sneak out our bedroom windows to go sleep at the neighbors'. I remember once or twice, Dad stomped out of the house in a rage, and we locked the door behind him. He came back with a sledgehammer and started yelling that he was going to break the door down. Somebody called the police on him and the squad cars arrived, lights flashing, to put an end to the embarrassing and frightening spectacle.

I don't ever remember my dad apologizing for any of it, either. In fact, nobody ever mentioned the episodes— ever. I guess it was supposed to be like it never happened. I am sure there were happy times with my dad when he was sober, but the damage wreaked inside me was real. *Why am I so messed up? What's wrong with me?* The questions ground at my insides, day after day, but I couldn't find any answers. Eventually, just to survive, I learned to shut my emotions down. I tried to make myself not care. The trouble with repressed anger and guilt, though, is that it's like radioactive waste. It just lies there, sometimes for decades, waiting for a chance to leak out of its container.

Fortunately, I experienced an incredible reconciliation in my relationship with my dad in the years prior to his death. But during those years in between, I felt this burning need inside to prove that I was okay—and somehow redeem myself. Most of us will do just about anything to meet those deepest longings for significance and security. Mine was tethered to performance.

Especially before coming to know the Lord, my life was one long search for approval. I was constantly trying to be good enough and stay busy enough to quiet the voice in my heart that almost continually whispered into my ear that I was messed up, lazy, and unworthy. Even after surrendering my life to Jesus, I continued to struggle with the legacy of a childhood bereft of a father's approval. Though I achieved my goals of becoming both a PGA Tour professional and a Bible study leader on the pro circuit, I was still, in many ways, "doing religion" instead of walking with Jesus. I often felt my faith was hollow at the center.

Frankly, I was worn out trying to be a sold-out believer. I was performance-driven, trying to please God and live a life acceptable to him, but I always fell short. I just couldn't live up to the expectations I felt God had of me, and I felt offensive to him. I kept asking myself, "What's wrong with you, Wally? Why can't you do this right?" I felt guilt and shame continually, and I even struggled to simply say the name of Jesus out loud.

Still, God sent many beautiful, caring people into my life and graciously offered me many signposts along the way. I truly wanted to be an authentic believer, so I never stopped praying and studying. I was continually reading everything I could find on how to best live the Christian life, listening to anyone who seemed to have some of the answers I was seeking.

I was still, in many ways, "doing religion" instead of walking with Jesus.

At the height of my striving, I picked up a book by USC professor and theologian Dallas Willard called *The Spirit of the Disciplines*. As I read the book, I was challenged again to review my life and see how I measured up to being a genuine follower of Christ. In my mind, I had a picture of sold-out believers: they were diligent in prayer and disciplined in studying the Word of God, in helping the poor, in fasting—all of those areas of my life where I felt that I fell short of achieving any consistent level of success. I kept thinking that if I practiced these disciplines hard enough, I might get to a place where I met God's expectations for me.

When I finished Willard's book, I felt such a profound ache in my soul. I just knew I was not proficient in the spiritual disciplines he was describing. I knew I had somehow missed it, and that made me feel like even more of a failure. I felt I could never measure up to the kind of life I thought I had to live for God to be proud of me.

> Maybe there was a big difference between changing and being transformed.

However, I decided to go back and review the book. Maybe I had missed something. And nothing could be truer because that "something" leapt out from the preface at the very start of the book! These words opened the door to a whole new life: "When we call men and women to life in Christ Jesus, we are offering them the greatest opportunity of their lives—the opportunity of a vivid companionship with him, in which they will learn to be like him and live as he lived. This is that 'transforming friendship' explained by Leslie Weatherhead. We *meet* and *dwell* with Jesus and his Father in the disciplines for the spiritual life."[1]

The words *transforming friendship* seemed to leap off the page at me. Could this really be the answer that I was looking for—a way to know Jesus and be transformed by his friendship? Maybe there was a big difference between changing and being transformed. My focus had always been on trying to change in order to get more acceptable to God. I talked to others about the peace of God, but my heart was filled with such turmoil. The more I tried to change, the more frustrated and defeated I became.

But a transforming friendship? That was something I'd not learned much about. I had heard people talk about trusting Christ every day, about being in relationship with him, even about having a friendship with him. But somehow it all seemed so complicated and difficult to understand. A friendship with Jesus seemed so foreign

---

1   Dallas Willard, *The Spirit of the Disciplines* (San Francisco: HarperSanFrancisco, 1988), xi.

to me. I had always considered myself a slave for Jesus—a workhorse—and because of this, Jesus always seemed so unapproachable. What if all this discussion was just some spiritualized chatter to explain away the fact that knowing Christ in an intimate, personal way was not really a practical possibility for people today? Even worse, though, was the thought that it was indeed possible...and I was missing it.

3

THE DAY
EVERYTHING
CHANGED

I BECAME CONSUMED WITH CURIOSITY ABOUT this transforming friendship that Dallas Willard said Leslie Weatherhead explained. I thought, *If Dallas Willard has referred to Weatherhead, there must be something significant about this guy. But who is he?* And what if it meant I could have a friendship with Jesus that was as real, as daily, and as immediate as my friendships with the people I saw each day? What if I could talk to Jesus just like I talked to a golfing buddy or a best friend, or like my wife might talk to a girlfriend? What if I could have a relationship with the Master that was as close, present, and surprising as any personal relationship in my life?

By doing some Internet research, I found to my surprise that Weatherhead wasn't a modern-day person at all. He had pastored a church in downtown London from the 1920s to the 1940s, and he also had a career as a psychiatrist. It turns out that in his later years, he'd held bizarre and very controversial views on some major tenets of the Christian faith, but there is no denying that God has used his first book, *The Transforming Friendship*, to impact a number of lives—mine included. Written back in 1929, the book was hard to find, but I located a used copy at a bookstore in Wisconsin and ordered it online. I couldn't wait to get my hands on the book. Maybe it would be the key that would finally unlock the door to a real, everyday friendship with the Savior. That would be the greatest treasure I could imagine!

> What if I could have a relationship
> with the Master that was as close,
> present, and surprising as any
> personal relationship in my life?

A few days later, I held *The Transforming Friendship* in my hands. My eyes were drawn to some words printed across the bottom of the cover: "The reality of the presence of Jesus among people like ourselves." It was almost like an electric current was coming out of the book and coursing into my body.

Was this the secret I had been missing all these years?

I've developed what has become a long-standing habit of getting up quite early to read and journal. The morning after I got this little red book was no exception. It was about 5:00 a.m. when I drifted into my den with my cup of coffee, settled down into my reading chair, and opened my newly acquired book.

The first words I saw when I began reading the prologue captured my mind. They set the stage for the following two hours—which would become the most enriching two hours of my life up to that point. The author wrote, "What we need as we embark on this quest of Christ is to get a picture of Him clearly in our minds."[2]

He had me right there. I knew I didn't have a clear picture of Jesus in my mind. Somehow, even after all these

---

2   Leslie Weatherhead, *The Transforming Friendship* (New York: Abingdon Press, 1929), 11.

years as a believer, Jesus existed for me as some kind of mystical Jewish-rabbi-ghost floating around in my mind. I realized that Western society had done little to dispel my confusion over Jesus' physical appearance—Sunday school pictures offer an Anglo-Saxon Jesus with a beard and long robe, stained-glass cathedral windows give us a distant and often stern-looking Englishman, and the Renaissance painters portrayed Jesus as an Italian. Of course, these artists all saw Jesus in the context of *their* world. But how did I view him, and how would he look if he were here today?

The truth is, I'd given Jesus the disposition of my father—demanding and impossible to please. I realized I'd spent my adult life holding on to a flawed picture of Jesus. I had been trying desperately to find my significance— proving my worth—in all the things I was doing for Christ, instead of getting my significance from his relationship with me.

Again and again I had tried to relate to him but never felt that he was approachable, especially when I blew it and found myself hiding in shame and self-contempt.

The book went on to dispel those mystical and ancient mental images of Jesus and to urge readers to imagine what he would look like today if he had come to live among us.

After all, when he showed up on the scene in Nazareth two thousand years ago, he had walked and talked and looked like the rest of the people living in that time and place.

As I was reading, the author shared a glimpse into the transforming friendship he experienced with Jesus in his own life. He described what happened one evening after arriving home from his church:

I have come home from some meetings thoroughly tired and disappointed and disillusioned. I have settled down in an armchair with bitterness in my veins instead of blood. There was a desire to write a letter calculated to crush one's opponent, and phrases which would silence him thronged on to the threshold of the mind. I was too tired to pray, too tired to stir up any desire to pray, and then I tried an experiment. I relaxed the body and relaxed the mind, left, as it were, the door of the mind ajar. There was very little more than a vague longing for the coming of the Friend, that Friend who understands, who understands our worst moments without losing belief in our best. And then something happened. The peace which is indescribable flooded the whole spirit; a hush which is ineffable quieted the mind. I have never seen a vision, I have never heard a voice, but I have felt that the last thing I wanted to do was to write the letter, and the last words I wanted to use were those which would have brought the pride of an opponent down to the dust. And there is only one explanation of such an experience. God's greatest gift to men was given and accepted. The Friend *came*.[3]

Sitting in my study that morning, in a pool of light in the midst of a darkened house, I stared at that last word. Italicized for emphasis, it leaned forward, like a child straining to peer around the door frame on Christmas morning.

Could it really be that simple?

This was exactly what I was looking for! I was seized by an incredible, burning desire to know Jesus as my Friend. It was as if Jesus was saying, "I'm ready to show you who I need to be to you in order for you to know me in this new way. Are you ready to find out?"

I decided right then to try to duplicate the experiment. Already in my favorite armchair, I simply laid my

---

3   Ibid., 28.

head back, closed my eyes, and sought to meet this real Friend—Jesus, my Savior and Lord, but in a new light. I was so intrigued by the idea of Jesus actually being alive today, as a real person just like you or me. Where would he be, and what would he look like today? *Show me, Jesus,* I thought. *I'm ready!*

A picture entered my mind. I was standing on the fringe of the practice green at the Disney World Magnolia Golf Course. As I scanned the people on the green, I suddenly spotted Jesus. He was wearing FootJoy shoes, khaki pants, a white golf shirt, and a blue Cubs cap. (This was appropriate, I thought, since nobody has more of a heart for the underdog than a diehard Cubs fan!) He was leaning on his new two-ball putter, watching a junior golfer practice three-footers.

Wow, that's really him! I thought. *He's clear as day. He's a golfer, he's a teacher, and he loves kids—just like me! I can talk to this guy!* I felt an instant connection with Jesus in my heart.

Then in my mind's eye, I saw Jesus turn and take a step toward me, and all of a sudden I experienced his very real presence right next to me, standing beside the arm of my chair in my study.

I cracked my eyes open a bit and looked to the side. I could still imagine the creases in his khaki pants as he stood there next to me.

Then a realization hit me. He had been there all along, but I just never saw him as a real person. So I opened my eyes, turned in his direction, and said out loud, "Hi. I've missed you all these years."

> For the first time, he was both holy
> and wholly approachable, and there
> was no fear or need to impress.

I began to simply talk with him in that moment, like one friend to another. I spoke with him like he was the kind of person he actually is—someone who is up-to-date and understands what's going on in the world and in my life. He seemed warm, as if he were welcoming me to receive the gift of his friendship. I began to imagine Jesus as all of my closest and dearest friends wrapped up into one person and multiplied by a million. For the first time, he was both holy and wholly approachable, and there was no fear or need to impress.

Of course, all of this was a bit difficult to grasp because I had so many misconceptions of what this relationship was really all about. I had so much to learn about being in this new companionship with Jesus, the true Friend! But the more I studied the life of Jesus and practiced being in his presence, the more this new gift of friendship presented a life-changing transformation of my heart and mind. It was an incredible experience, and it became even more real and precious to me in the days that followed.

I began reading the Gospels with fresh eyes, and it became apparent that Jesus was someone people were eager to follow, someone who rarely condemned. He saw the deepest yearnings inside the men and women who sought him, and just being with him seemed to give people the courage and confidence to live out those possibilities. I think of impulsive, headstrong Peter, who walked and talked with Jesus and revered him as Lord, and whose companionship with Jesus helped him grow into the kind of man who could lead the early church. Friendship with Jesus made men and women want to be just like him and to believe that likeness was actually within reach.

What if that were the friendship Jesus offers today? Could it be that people often miss the great gift of companionship with Christ after accepting Jesus as their personal Savior and Lord? The book went on to suggest that many of us get quickly trapped into focusing on one of two directions: either we are caught up in a flurry of performance as we try to live the Christian life in service to God, or we set our minds on acquiring more knowledge in the hope that with wisdom we will gain holiness. Of course, both of these paths leave us empty, because we've overlooked what Jesus came to give us. In essence, we leapfrog over Jesus and dive into the shallow pond of cultural Christianity, jumping from one lily pad of misconception to the next.

> People often miss the great gift of companionship with Christ after accepting Jesus as their personal Savior and Lord.

We have missed the gift of simple friendship, even though that friendship was the first thing Jesus offered his disciples before he ever taught them to minister or schooled them in theology.

I could certainly relate to this conundrum. For years, people have told me I have more energy than anybody they've ever seen. It's a fact: left to my own devices, I can go from one project to another, one tournament to another, one coaching session to another, one event to another—never looking around, never pausing, never stopping to reflect or question or savor the moment. Like a kid on a merry-go-round, stretching and reaching as hard as he can for the brass ring so he can get another free ride, I never enjoyed one moment of the ride itself.

In my lifetime of striving to win approval and acceptance by focusing on performance, I knew that even the most committed believers in Jesus fall into the trap of making service or a mastery of theological knowledge the main focus instead of first resting in a friendship. I, too, had spent most of my life as a "human doing" rather than a human being.

For years I had been caught up in seeking answers through other people's methods and experiences. Three ways to be a great father…ten steps to handle anger…eight steps to deal with damaged emotions… My shelves were overflowing with books that were full of important truths, but I tried to apply them through self-determination and hard work. I saw periods of change in my life, but they never lasted because I'd missed the real truth: Jesus, the one true King, was alive and present and seeking my friendship as a brother and companion.

The fact is, most people—myself included—miss the second most important conversation they are meant to have. The first conversation is accepting Jesus as Savior; the second one is accepting Jesus as Friend. I believe this is a conversation that is meant to begin right after our life with Christ gets started—and it's never meant to end! It's a process of thanking Jesus for the gift of his salvation, and then welcoming his offer to walk by his side from here on out.

> Instead of having a mere relationship
> with Jesus, I was beginning to learn
> how to experience his ever-present
> and interactive companionship.

I look back now and recall that this was never clearly presented to me. In fact, I don't think I've ever heard or read anything about this most important step, which is really the foundation of discipleship. Instead of learning how to be a disciple by living in ongoing conversation and friendship with Jesus, we try to be discipled without

Christ, following principles we pick up about Christianity rather than following him.

Four months later, in April, I was at Augusta National, and the real-life scene developed that I described in the first chapter. I realized that seeing the actor who had played Jesus in a movie—someone who looked just like most of the people on the golf course that day—was such a fitting image for this exciting new spiritual quest I had begun in the past few months. In fact, I later realized that Jim Caviezel looked remarkably similar to the Jesus I had seen in my vision on that wonderful winter morning four months earlier in my home office.

What an incredible confirmation was that glimpse of "Jesus" on the green! I was coming to see that God was doing something very new in my life with him. Instead of having a mere relationship with Jesus, I was beginning to learn how to experience his ever-present and interactive companionship.

4

THe CHair EXPerimeNT

AS YOU MIGHT IMAGINE, MY FIRST TASTE of Jesus' real
presence that early morning in my den only made me want
to experience more of him! I began devouring the book
like it was a huge, hot-fudge sundae, each word sweet and
delicious. In the second chapter, called "The Reality of the
Friendship," the author poses an intriguing question and
then answers it with a powerful story.

> Can we enter into this friendship? We can. We can, as
> Brother Lawrence said, "practice the presence of God,"
> but the only way I know of practicing the presence of
> God is by practicing the presence of Jesus, who makes
> God credible and real, and entering into the transform-
> ing friendship which He offers.

An old Scotsman lay very ill, and his minister came to visit him. As the minister sat down on a chair near the bedside, he noticed on the other side of the bed another chair placed at such an angle as to suggest that a visitor had just left it.

"Well, Donald," said the minister, glancing at the chair, "I see I am not your first visitor."

The Scotsman looked up in surprise, so the minister pointed to the chair.

"Ah!" said the sufferer, "I'll tell you about the chair. Years ago I found it impossible to pray. I often fell asleep on my knees I was so tired. And if I kept awake I could not control my thoughts from wandering. One day I was so worried I spoke to my old minister about it. He told me not to worry about kneeling down. 'Just sit down,' he said, 'and put a chair opposite you, imagine that Jesus is in it and talk to Him as you would to a friend.' And," the Scotsman added, "I have been doing that ever since. So now you know why the chair is standing like that."

A week later the daughter of the old Scot drove up to the minister's house and knocked at his door. She was shown into the study, and when the minister came in she could hardly restrain herself.

"Father died in the night," she sobbed. "I had no idea death could be so near. I had just gone to lie down for an hour or two. He seemed to be sleeping so comfortably. And when I went back he was dead. He hadn't moved since I saw him before, except *that his hand was out on the empty chair at the side of the bed*. Do you understand?"

"Yes," said the minister, "I understand." The Scotsman, not by intellect or will, but by an imagination which had become faith, had accepted the gift of a friendship and made the Master real. Truly "our fellowship is with the Father and with His Son Jesus Christ."

The reality of the transforming friendship is reached not through argument but through experience.[4]

As I read this moving story, it became clear to me that the old Scotsman had grasped the most elementary principle of faith which Jesus talked about—the faith of a little child. I wondered, *Why do we make it so complicated?*

Reading these words about the old Scotsman and the chair, I once again felt an irresistible desire to try this new idea for myself. I looked at the swivel desk chair on the

---

4   Leslie Weatherhead, *The Transforming Friendship*, 46–47.

other side of my office and imagined Jesus sitting there, looking at me. It was uncomfortable at first—I felt almost silly for trying—but I did it anyway because I wanted so much to believe in the reality of Christ's presence and friendship. In order to get there, I had to let myself imagine it really was true.

A phrase from the story emboldened me—the old Scotsman had "imagination which had become faith." By an exercise of imagination, the man had grown into a faith in Christ's intimate presence that was strong and unshakable. It was so strong that even in the moment of death, his impulse was to reach for the hand of the Friend who was seated in the chair beside his bed.

> In order to get there, I had to let myself imagine it really was true.

Could it be that our imagination—guided by the Holy Spirit—is the natural starting point for our faith? In order to grow into a firm belief that Jesus is real and with us today, we need only imagine him walking by our side throughout our day. When we sense his presence alongside of us, guiding us, speaking to us, offering companionship, then our experience verifies its truth. Our childlike imagination becomes a grown-up faith.

Interactions with my seven grandchildren brought home to me the idea of this kind of friendship with Jesus. It is so easy for the little ones to kneel by their bedside in prayer, imagining Jesus right there beside them. Untarnished by the jaded and cynical perspective of adults, children can easily grasp the gift of his friendship and sense his presence beside them. Of course, my grandchildren also imagine Santa Claus and the tooth fairy showing up in the middle of the night, but as they grow up, the fantasy of fairies and made-up stories will fall away, while the truth of a real and vital relationship with Jesus can stay with them forever.

I wanted that kind of imagination—the kind that grows into a strong faith in the living, real presence of Jesus.

Now, don't get me wrong—I know the New Age movement and other religions have claimed and tainted the concept of imagination and visualization as the key to approaching a "higher power," but who created our capacity to imagine? And if our imagination, under the authority of our Creator, allows us to embrace the truth of Jesus and his offer of friendship, then it becomes a life-changing, faith-filled practice.

So I began picturing my Friend sitting across from me in the chair and myself talking to him. Giving him a place to sit and a space to occupy in my world made his presence even more real to me than on that previous morning when I "saw" him in my mind on the putting green at Disney World. This simple, practical method of imagining Jesus sitting in a chair across from me helped me to communicate even better with my Friend.

You can have imagination without faith, but you can't really live your faith without imagination. It became clear to me that my imagination was not being used as an escape but was becoming a gateway into reality.

Have I mentioned that focusing on anything, for any length of time, is not my specialty? As someone who has had a lifelong struggle with ADHD, I am often easily distracted. During conversations with my good friend Bill Stephens, when my mind begins to drift, I often hear him say, "Armstrong, are you listening to me?" Because Bill and I are such close friends, I can receive his mild and gentle rebuke, knowing it is wrapped up in love. In the same way, when I am enjoying time with Jesus and my mind begins to get off track—*I wonder if I've covered all the details for that golf event later today. And why hasn't that guy called me back about Friday's conference?*—I become aware of Jesus' loving voice saying, "Armstrong, are you listening to me?" He wants me to enjoy his presence, to trust him with my worries, and to have faith in his willingness to walk beside me each day.

> I wanted that kind of imagination—the
> kind that grows into a strong faith in
> the living, real presence of Jesus.

There were so many amazing experiences during those early months of learning to imagine Jesus sitting across from me in the chair with open arms and a warm smile. But sometimes it was very difficult to look over at the chair if I felt shame or guilt. I know very well the words of Romans 8:1—that there is no condemnation for those who are in Christ Jesus. Still, I would beat myself up and pour condemnation on myself whenever I sinned. As I look back on those times now, I see that I was much harder on myself than Jesus ever was. And the Holy Spirit began steering me toward the true Jesus—the Savior who gently corrected and loved me through the process. Those early morning hours when I practiced this new experiment brought me into the fullness of life and the companionship Jesus had always promised, but that I'd never before been able to find.

The more I practiced being in his presence, the more I began to overcome these false, dysfunctional views of God that I'd carried for so long. Why had it been so hard for me to let Jesus love me? Little by little, I allowed Jesus to love me as I learned to look at him and imagine his arms open and ready to give me a hug. And the interesting thing is, I learned to also love myself as I let him love me. This happened not by claiming the truth of Romans 8:1, but by sensing the firm yet loving words of Jesus directly.

> As I look back on those times now,
> I see that I was much harder on
> myself than Jesus ever was.

For example, I remember sitting in my chair one morning filled with contempt and shame, having a really hard time looking over at the chair where Jesus sat across from me. And then my heart heard these words: "Wally, don't do that to yourself. There's no condemnation. Listen to me now—no condemnation."

Those words penetrated my soul and were received with such humble joy. While this is still one of my greatest battle areas, that moment of love and forgiveness helped me learn to accept the peace he offers and receive his intimacy and care. Each time this happened, it was a step further in putting on my new self and renewing my mind, just as 2 Corinthians 4:16 says: "Therefore we do not lose heart, but though our outer man is decaying, yet our inner man is being renewed day by day."

And then, before I knew it, I was talking to Jesus in the car too. I would be driving along, preoccupied with my thoughts, and it would occur to me that Jesus had not stayed behind in the den when I left my house that morning. He had come with me out of the house and was sitting right next to me in the car! Instead of puzzling alone over the thoughts inside my head, I realized I could engage him again in this new light of friendship about whatever was on my mind. It was just how I might talk with a friend sitting there with me in the passenger seat.

I remember driving down toward Atlanta one day after visiting some friends in the mountains of North Carolina.

It was a beautiful day, and I was enjoying the magnificent view while listening to some praise music on the radio. Then all of a sudden it hit me that my Friend Jesus was with me in the car, and I began to enjoy the view and the music with him. I was finally grasping the joy of the Lord that is spoken of in the Scriptures. The joy comes from basking in the warm embrace of Jesus' presence and simply enjoying life with him. I think this is what the psalmist meant when he said to "delight yourself in the LORD; and He will give you the desires of your heart" (Psalm 37:4).

> The key is that he does want to speak to us—to you—today. In your own language, just as a friend would speak. We simply need to take the time to listen.

I had heard my pastor, Joel Hunter, tell stories many times about talking to Jesus out loud in the car. I had always thought that sounded crazy! Yet there I was, beginning to do it. The experience of talking with Jesus in the chair across from me in my den had sharpened my imagination so that I soon could see him coming and going with me everywhere.

Another time I was rushing to meet a friend at Starbucks when I found myself stuck in a terrible traffic jam, just a half-mile from my destination and running late. I could see the Starbucks up ahead, but I was stuck—not only in traffic but in the mire of my quickly building frustration and anxiety. Then I became aware of my Friend, speaking as a true friend would: "What's going on with you? What's the rush? Don't you think I have everything under control? Lighten up on the wheel, take a deep breath, and realize that it is all okay." What a relief to hear the truth of his affirmation and loving rebuke, spoken in plain English as if he were right there next to me.

The key is that he does want to speak to us—to you—today. In your own language, just as a friend would speak. We simply need to take the time to listen.

Now, please don't get the wrong idea. If the idea of imagining Jesus sitting across from you in a chair or seated with you in your car doesn't speak to your mind and heart, maybe that isn't the best way for you to approach your friendship with him. Not long ago, I met a woman who said Jesus became real to her one day on the back porch of her house.

It's not about the chair. It's about making a place in your world to connect with and fully enjoy your Friend, Jesus. Seek him in ways that make you feel comfortable and safe—for I am convinced that he will come and meet you. There's nothing magical about a chair.

In fact, there's nothing magical about any of this. It isn't magic or mind tricks or some sort of spiritual trance you should be pursuing here. And it isn't audible voices or visions that we're seeking here, but a *knowing*, a sensing of his presence, and a chance to hear him with our heart. This story is about coming to see Jesus clearly as the real and living person he is. He is the one who lives in your world today and wants to spend time with you, listening to you and teaching you everything he wants you to learn.

Isn't it interesting that in the gospel of John, chapter 15, Jesus tells this very thing to his best friends?

"Greater love has no one than this: to lay down one's life for one's friends. You are my friends if you do what I command. I no longer call you servants, because a servant does not know his master's business. Instead,

I have called you friends, for everything that I learned from my Father I have made known to you. You did not choose me, but I chose you and appointed you so that you might go and bear fruit—fruit that will last—and so that whatever you ask in my name the Father will give you. This is my command: Love each other" (John 15:13–17 NIV).

Here he is, two thousand years later, personally teaching us the same truths! I know you may find it hard to believe, as I still sometimes do, that he really wants to know you and be known by you. But it's true. He wants, in fact, what any friend worthy of the name wants: your companionship.

> It's about making a place in your world to connect with and fully enjoy your Friend, Jesus.

5

HOW IT WAS MEANT TO BE

A FEW YEARS AGO, MY WIFE AND I SPENT Easter weekend with our daughter, her husband, and our granddaughters at St. Augustine Beach, a quaint town on the northeast coast of Florida. That Saturday, when I woke early and went around the corner to Starbucks for my morning coffee, I followed a prompting to call my friend Father Joseph Girzone. Joe is a retired Catholic priest who divides his time between New York and Maryland, leading retreats for people who desire to know Jesus better. He is best known for writing the *Joshua* series of books. Those closest to him know of his deep friendship with Jesus and his ability to lead others deeper into their own friendship with him.

To my delight, Joe picked up the phone when I called, and we proceeded to talk for a couple hours. Father Joe was excited to hear of my newfound friendship with Jesus, and he said the reality of this friendship was really nothing new. Joe shared with me that he has spent years studying the writings of the church fathers, and particularly those of the first-century believers. He's learned a great deal about how the church grew before the New Testament writings were ever collected and canonized as sacred Scripture.

You see, before the Bible as we know it came to be—something that didn't happen until the fourth century—the church had already grown into a force that would completely change the world. How did that happen? How did those early followers of Jesus crop up everywhere without the Bible to teach them or huge churches with teaching pastors, worship pastors, and children's programs to equip them?

It was one person telling another person what it was like to know Jesus, and then that person experiencing the same resurrected Jesus for themselves and passing the story along to someone else.

Father Joe told me what he'd learned about how people came to know Jesus in those early days. The apostles went into different towns across the vast Roman Empire, befriended the people they met there, and told them everything they knew about Jesus and what it was like to know him. In essence, they equipped more apprentices to follow this Jesus whom they loved so much. As more and more people came to know Jesus, the church began to grow simply through the continued sharing of stories. It was one person telling another person what it was like to know Jesus, and then that person experiencing the same resurrected Jesus for themselves and passing the story along to someone else.

I could imagine two items topping the list of "Most Important Things" for the apostles to teach people about Jesus: who Jesus was as a person, and how to experience him as real right now. The first disciples of Jesus, after all, had the privilege of walking and talking with him every day for three whole years. They knew his mannerisms, his way of speaking, and his touch. They knew what he was like in conversation and what it was like to receive his gaze. They knew his laughter, his smile, and his tears. They knew what made him the kind of person the crowds would follow and the religious leaders would despise. The disciples knew what it was like to be his friend, and it was this dynamic friendship with him that made all the difference in their lives. At some point, the disciples must have realized that this was the way mankind was meant to live.

In Father Joe's book *A Portrait of Jesus*, he writes,

> He [Jesus] shared His life, which He wanted His followers to be a part of. It was intimate and personal. He told the people His father wanted them to be His children and His friends. When Christianity put the trappings of royal courts into its structure, it made itself foreign to the mind and spirit of Jesus. Jesus knew He was King, but that was not what He wanted people to see in Him…. All Jesus wanted from people was their friendship, and for them to establish a warm relationship with His father.[5]

To invite all these people who had never met Jesus to follow him completely, the disciples would have had to create the clearest picture possible of what this Jesus was like and what he said and did. They would have had to help people understand the quality and depth of Jesus as a person. They would have had to translate the essence of his life and

---

5   Joseph F. Girzone, *A Portrait of Jesus* (New York: Doubleday 1998), 141.

teachings so that following Jesus was the most obvious and desirable thing to do in this world.

What it really came down to was that if those listeners hadn't been given a real sense of Jesus, what reason would they have had to follow him? Many of the earliest believers were persecuted and killed in horrendous ways for their faith. (If you want to learn more about this, read Hebrews 10:32–34.) It seems to me that there had to be a much more powerful force alive in those early believers than a person can get from just hearing stories about a good man who lived and died and had some insightful things to say about life.

> The disciples knew what it was like to be his friend, and it was this dynamic friendship with him that made all the difference in their lives.

It also became clear to me that the disciples would have had to teach people that it was still possible to experience a living friendship with Jesus. We know that a relationship with Jesus continued to be an option since he promised to be with his followers until the end of the age (Matthew 28:20).

Jesus also told Peter on the beach that early morning after his resurrection, "Follow Me" (John 21:19, 22). But how was Peter to follow someone who was no longer there? What was that relationship supposed to look like now? And how were they to teach other people to enjoy it?

I have come to understand that the times Jesus spent with his followers *after* his resurrection were used specifically to train them in this new way of friendship—a friendship no longer dependent on his physical presence. Think about it—the disciples were together, sharing a meal, and suddenly Jesus was there among them, talking with them, eating with them. Two people were on their way to Emmaus, and suddenly Jesus was walking alongside them in companionship. He spoke words of peace to his disciples in the Upper Room, then they saw him on the seashore and again near the town of Bethany.

They were learning how to be aware of him always, whether they could see and hear him or not.

His followers were learning how to be aware of him always, whether they could see and hear him or not. By going in and out of their presence, always appearing with complete knowledge of what they were thinking and discussing before he arrived, Jesus was training them to realize that he was with them at all times. He was training them to be mindful of him and expectant of his presence. And soon, when he no longer physically appeared to them, this practiced awareness of his ongoing presence tutored them to listen with their inward ears to his voice.

This was such a key development for the disciples because it not only taught them how to continue as followers of Jesus themselves but also how to help others do the same. These disciples were charged with the responsibility of teaching the rest of the world about this ever-present Jesus and how to be his followers. They were to teach people how to experience each day in the presence of someone beyond the bounds of physical sight. In short, they were given the task of helping people develop spiritual sight—to engage this real, ever-present Jesus through their imagination and to experience his powerful life flowing in and through them as a result.

Do you remember a few years ago when the WWJD phenomenon swept the country? It seemed everywhere you looked, people were wearing those braided nylon bracelets with WWJD woven into them. The idea is great: always ask yourself, in every situation, "What would Jesus do?" In fact, that question was the basis for Charles Sheldon's 1896 book, *In His Steps*, which has transformed and inspired several generations of believers.

> Instead of wondering what Jesus would do, what if you could just ask him directly?

But that question, as well-intentioned as it is, usually gets us to focus on ourselves—our own power to figure out what Jesus would do and then, in our own power again, to attempt to go do it. But instead of wondering what Jesus would do, what if you could just ask him directly? And instead of doing it alone, what if you could have him with you all along, showing you how and giving you the strength to carry it out? This is what those familiar words of Matthew 11:28, 30 really mean, which say, "Come to Me, all who are weary and heavy-laden, and I will give you rest…. For My yoke is easy and My burden is light."

For most of my life, I had pursued my spiritual life just like I had pursued excelling at my golf game. It takes years and years of discipline and hard work to achieve the level of performance required to compete on the PGA Tour. In my mind, it would take the same hard work to achieve the level of "Super Christian." The idea of the "rest" that Jesus offered in Matthew chapter 11? It just wasn't part of my fabric.

I see now that there are thousands of people who call themselves Christians who aren't really following Christ. Calling yourself a Christian today has become just a label. Do you think Jesus would have labeled himself a Christian? I think he would have simply identified himself as a follower of his Father. He was living out the essence of his relationship with his Father and offering us the chance to follow him in the same way he followed his dad.

There were times in my life when I felt close to Jesus, but only when I felt my life was clean enough for him to be able to associate with me. In fact, at one point I got caught up in the theological view that unless I had confessed all my known sin to God, I couldn't have a close relationship with him. I had to get "cleaned up" before he could deal with me. I poured my energy into achieving good-enough status, instead of pursuing a real and interactive friendship with Jesus based upon his unconditional love for me.

The great news is that these aren't just "what if" scenarios! Our relationship with Jesus really can be this way—a friendship with the great I AM, a friend with whom we can talk, who relates to us in every way and is interested in all the details of our lives. It was always meant to be this way.

Father Joe conveys this idea beautifully in his bestselling *Joshua* series, where a modern-day Jesus figure moves into a small town. He looks and talks just like one of them, though at first he mystifies the people with his simple, quiet ways. Soon, though, he begins to have an extraordinary effect on everyone who comes in contact with him, and their lives are transformed by his incredible warmth and the way he always focuses on others. He loves even the outcasts, and lives are transformed by simply spending time with him.

If you believe the truth about Jesus' life, death, and resurrection and you believe his promise to never leave us or forsake us, then consider this: Jesus is a real and living person. He did not stay in the grave on that weekend of his death but came to life again. He presented himself alive to the disciples, and he is still alive today!

> The way we relate to Jesus and live
> in the world depends entirely on
> the picture of him that we carry.

Just as the disciples worked primarily to help their listeners gain as clear a picture of Jesus as possible in their minds, so is the primary aim of this book to set you on the path to forming that same clear picture in your own mind. This clear picture is so important because the way we relate to Jesus and live in the world depends entirely on the picture of him that we carry.

For instance, my own encounter with Jesus through the experiments I began at the very beginning of this journey taught me that I'd been carrying faulty pictures of Jesus around with me for years. For thirty-six years of believing in him, in fact, I'd developed many misconceptions and blurry images. These affected everything I did in my efforts to live as one of his followers! Many of those years were spent focusing on getting the doctrines right rather than seeing and knowing Jesus in this new, dynamic way. But slowly, as I spent time with him and allowed him to access and activate my imagination, Jesus graciously began to direct my attention to different pictures of himself. They were pictures rooted in his truth and his real personality. These new pictures began to set me on a new path. I wish for you this same new path full of clearer pictures!

We don't have the twelve disciples here to teach us this clear picture of Jesus in the same way they taught those believers in the early days of the church. But what we *do* have are their four distinct accounts of the life of Christ from the New Testament. We can get to know the Jesus they knew by studying all they had to say about him.

The apostle John writes in his letter to all those who will follow after him through the centuries that they may experience the same friendship with Jesus that he knew. The Message paraphrase clearly gives us this picture in 1 John 1:1–3.

From the very first day, we were there, taking it all in—we heard it with our own ears, saw it with our own eyes, verified it with our own hands. The Word of Life appeared right before our eyes; we saw it happen! And now we're telling you in most sober prose that what we witnessed was, incredibly, this: The infinite Life of God himself took shape before us. We saw it, we heard it, and now we're telling you so you can experience it along with us, this experience of communion with the Father and his Son, Jesus Christ.

It doesn't get much clearer than this. And what's more, we can also learn from Jesus directly!

That's the place I began nine years ago when I realized I needed a clearer picture of Jesus. Previously, I had awakened early in the morning to read the Bible and journal on a regular basis. I had a real thirst to know God, but my Bible reading was usually done either in an attempt to learn more about God (rather than to know God directly) or to make myself a better person.

Though learning about God and wanting to be a better person sound like positive desires, they kept my faith in a carefully managed box and never gave me a chance to know or be known by God. I understood how much Jesus loved me, and yet I felt there was still not a friendly connection. I was working so hard to please him but certainly could not imagine Jesus offering me companionship.

> My faith had been contained in a carefully
> managed box that never gave me a
> chance to know or be known by God.

This new experience with Jesus gave me that something more. First, it crystallized the person of Jesus in my mind. It made him real to me. And second, it helped the Bible become a real and living tutor in my life that complemented my relationship with Jesus and continues to show me more about him.

This happened because I began to read the Bible and imagined Jesus sitting right next to me. As I read its pages each day with Jesus, I started to ask him questions about what I was reading. Just as he did with the two disciples on the road to Emmaus (Luke 24:13–27), I felt that Jesus opened up the Scriptures to me.

I believe the author of the Bible himself wants to speak to all of us personally through his Word. And of course, nothing he says to us will ever contradict the truth of the Scriptures taken as a whole.

One morning I was struggling again with feelings of shame and my old formula of "human doing" to be good enough to approach the throne of God. Then I heard him clearly speaking to my heart, "Don't let that old garbage get in the way of receiving my love. I went to the cross for you, my brother, so that we could have this time to enjoy together, now and throughout eternity. This is only a glimpse of the ultimate moment when you will see me face-to-face."

Those words were like a hug from a dear friend and became an important step in renewing my mind and embracing a new walk—one of friendship and loyalty and integrity—with Jesus.

Just as the disciples needed to teach others how to be in relationship with Jesus, so the second aim of this book is to help you become aware of the ongoing companionship of Jesus throughout your daily life.

Although the practice of the chair experiment increases the clarity of our picture of Jesus, the chair is not the only place Jesus wants to meet us. He wants us to grow in our grasp of his continuous presence, just as he taught the disciples to do in those post-resurrection appearances and has taught millions of believers throughout the centuries.

The good news is that I have found this begins to happen more naturally as we continue the practice of meeting with Jesus in this way each day and accepting the friendship he offers.

6

Jesus, the First Disciple

FROM THE VERY FIRST DAY I SAT WITH JESUS and opened up
the New Testament, keeping a notebook by my side and
a pen in hand, I asked Jesus to reveal to me the true picture of who he is and the invitation he offers to be his
follower and his friend. One of those first conversations
with Jesus began with the question, "Who was your best
friend?" I figured I could learn a lot about making Jesus
my closest friend by studying the example of his own closest friendship.

It wasn't long before I came to realize that Jesus' own
best friend was none other than his dad, our heavenly
Father! As a pair, they demonstrate a picture of total oneness, don't they? I remembered how often Jesus would get
up in the earliest hours of the morning to spend time with

his dad all alone. I remembered, too, how he told his disciples that everything he said to them came directly from the guidance of his Father and the conversations they'd shared together. There was a sense of deep communion between the two of them. They shared a rich fellowship that grew out of the time they spent together in real and honest dialogue on a regular basis. In fact, I have heard it said that the greatest work of Jesus' life was the time he spent alone with his Father. During that time, he was refreshed to do the rest of the work he'd been called to do.

> Jesus and his Father shared a rich fellowship
> that grew out of the time they spent together
> in real and honest dialogue on a regular basis.

I came to realize, too, that this close relationship Jesus shared with the Father made him the very first disciple of the faith. A disciple is a learner and a follower, and Jesus spent time with the Father each day to learn who the Father was and what he, Jesus, was to do and say on the Father's behalf in the world. He apprenticed himself to the Father through their relationship. And then each day, he lived, loved, and was guided and nurtured along through the companionship of his dad, who was right by his side.

Later still in this journey, I had another revelation that taught me just how close a relationship Jesus shared with his Father. It happened when I was thinking about that most difficult of all conversations Jesus ever shared with him: when he went to pray in the garden of Gethsemane. We learn in the Scriptures that Jesus was in such anguish about what lay ahead—his road to the cross—that he said to his Father that night, "If you are willing, take this cup from me; yet not my will, but yours be done" (Luke 22:42 NIV). After this prayer, we see that an angel comes to strengthen him, confirming the Father's will that he proceed upon this road, and Jesus begins sweating drops of blood (verses 43–44). It is as though, having received confirmation and strength from the angel, he knew he could not finish this road on his own. He needed a strength coming from beyond himself, which the Father provided for him.

I don't know about you, but I used to have a Sunday school picture in my head of that moment when Jesus knelt on the ground, his long robe flowing out behind him, his elbows perched on a rock, his hands folded, his eyes straining skyward in prayer. I imagined his prayer floating upward to the sky to reach God in heaven, but in my mind, God was so far removed from all Jesus felt in that moment. I imagined the Father with a bit of a frown on his face at hearing Jesus' prayer. I saw him holding out the emotionally distant expectation that Jesus should just man up, be strong, and do what he'd been sent down to earth to do.

> Everything I understood about the kind of friendship Jesus offers us changed from viewing those pictures of his close friendship with his Father.

But now, having realized their relationship was one of such intimacy—to the point that the Father was Jesus' very best friend and even sent an angel to give him strength during his time of greatest need—my sense of that moment in the garden began to change. As a father myself, I began to imagine what it would have been like for my own son to be in Jesus' shoes that night. If that were the case, I knew I would have wanted to be right there with my son in that garden on the last night of his freedom, throwing my arms around him, hugging him close to my chest, and letting him cry those tears onto my shoulder. I would not have wanted to let him go. I would have wanted him to know how much I loved him so there would be no doubt in his mind. I would have grieved deeply with him for what lay ahead and could not be avoided.

It would have been agony for me too.

Everything I understood about the kind of friendship Jesus offers us changed from viewing those pictures of his close friendship with his Father. I came to see that, for Jesus, talking to God was simply talking to his best friend. He considered the Father to be the closest person to him in the entire world. He knew the Father was near. He experienced the Father's care for him in all of their encounters. He shared the depth of his feelings with the Father and experienced the Father meeting him in those depths. He felt the Father's provision in his greatest moments of need.

And now, Jesus wants us to experience that same kind of intimacy. The apostle John tells us that our fellowship is with both the Father and the Son (1 John 1:3). Jesus prayed toward the end of his life that he would be in us as the

Father was in him (John 17:23). He also told his disciples that he calls us his friends because he has shared with us everything the Father told him (John 15:15). Clearly, Jesus offers us the chance to share with him the same kind of union he and the Father have known all along.

That's an incredible gift, isn't it? What would it look like for you to relate to God in this same way? How might you begin to allow yourself to experience this same depth of friendship with the Father and the Son that they're offering you right now?

Jesus makes this incredible union possible through the gift of the Holy Spirit. On the last night he was with his disciples, Jesus told them that a Helper, the Holy Spirit, would be coming in order to teach them all he had to say and to call to mind his words (John 14:26). These are the same words that were always spoken out of a place of union with the Father. When the Holy Spirit did come, he gave all the followers of Jesus a strength that was not their own. Other people marveled and finally concluded this power came from having been with Jesus (Acts 2:1–21; 4:8–13).

The Father, Jesus, and the Holy Spirit enjoy a wonderful, intimate, unique relationship. Scripture teaches us that God has no beginning and no end, which means that the triune

God—who is the Father, the Son Jesus, and the Holy Spirit— has always existed in relationship. This heavenly, celestial camaraderie has always been part of God's very being. One of the reasons Jesus came to earth was to provide a way for us to experience relationship with the only true, three-in-one, one-in-three God. Imagine a holy God interested in befriending us!

> Jesus offers us the chance to share with him the same kind of union he and the Father have known all along.

Jesus' life demonstrated how to live within this unique, interactive friendship. In fact, he said that he could only accomplish what he did because of his life-sustaining relationship with his own Father. Jesus challenges us to follow him and to live the same way—in fellowship with God now and forever.

When you think about it, building a community of brothers and sisters united in following Christ, led by the Holy Spirit, has always been God's goal on this earth. Jesus makes this clear in his prayer to the Father in John 17:1–11 (NIV).

"Father, the hour has come. Glorify your Son, that your Son may glorify you. For you granted him authority over all people that he might give eternal life to all those you have given him. Now this is eternal life: that they know you, the only true God, and Jesus Christ, whom you have sent. I have brought you glory on earth by finishing the work you gave me to do. And now, Father, glorify me in your presence with the glory I had with you before the world began.

"I have revealed you to those whom you gave me out of the world. They were yours; you gave them to me and they have obeyed your word. Now they know that everything you have given me comes from you. For I gave them the words you gave me and they accepted them. They knew with certainty that I came from you, and they believed that you sent me. I pray for them. I am not praying for the world, but for those you have given me, for they are yours. All I have is yours, and all you have is mine. And glory has come to me through them. I will remain in the world no longer, but they are still in the world, and I am coming to you. Holy Father, protect them by the power of your name, the name you gave me, so that they may be one as we are one."

The way this fellowship—this oneness—thrives is through the power of the Holy Spirit, who gives us the spiritual eyesight and insight to see life through a whole new pair of spectacles. Living by faith, in the oneness of our walk with Jesus, empowered by the Holy Spirit, we enjoy community with the Father and with our fellow man. This "kingdom living" perfectly fulfills what Jesus said was the greatest commandment: to love the Lord your God with all your heart and mind and soul, and to love your neighbor as yourself.

So how does this relationship begin for us? By understanding and accepting the ransom that Jesus offered through his death for us on the cross. He took our certificate of debt—our sin—and nailed it to the cross. He is not keeping score anymore. John 3:16 (NIV) states it so clearly: "For God so loved the world that he gave his one and only Son, that whoever believes in him shall not perish but have eternal life." This is the invitation into fellowship with God. His desire is for all those who receive the gift of eternal life to then live within the companionship of Jesus and his Father, the same way that Jesus lived with his Father on earth—as it was in heaven.

I have never seen the incredible truth of this concept better illustrated than in the case of my father. As I said earlier, life with him was not easy. When I gave my life to Christ, the great divide between my father and me became even greater. He viewed my faith as a crutch and called me weak and gullible. Later, though, when Dad was facing a surgery we knew might signal his last moments on earth, I just had to talk with him about the Lord. For the first time in our lives, Dad and I had a heart-to-heart discussion about the eternal life God offers.

"Wally, I'm not a bad person," he told me, and my heart sank. "I've always tried to do my best to take care of Mom and the family." I knew he was still relying on his own performance instead of God's forgiveness. Thankfully, we had several more years with Dad after that surgery, and during that time he began to read some of the faith-related books I'd given him and even read from the Bible. One night, just a few months before he died, my parents attended a Billy Graham crusade. That night he took my mother's hand and went forward to give his life to Christ. He told me later, "Billy said that when Christ enters your life, he takes the slate where he has been keeping a record of your sins and erases it. Not only that, he throws the slate away! Son, that's the kind of forgiveness I've needed."

What an incredible moment for us! Over the next few months, we saw Dad's health deteriorate, but his childlike faith blossomed. He was thrilled to discover the freedom and joy found in Christ living inside of him, transforming his life into something wonderful. Even though I was sad to see him go, I can't wait to see him in heaven someday!

> Being with Jesus, in communion with the Father, empowered and taught by the wisdom of the Holy Spirit—this is what the transforming friendship is all about.

My father lived his life in a concrete world, relying on sight and sound and touch. When he discovered the truth of Jesus right beside him, and as he saw Jesus through the eyes of his heart, my dad became a new man. It isn't surprising that so many of us find it difficult to imagine how we can live each day in the reality of this truth: being *in* Jesus and he in us. In fact, it is only through our imagination that we can grasp this reality.

Being with Jesus, in communion with the Father, empowered and taught by the wisdom of the Holy Spirit— this is what the transforming friendship is all about. And the amazing news is that it can begin right where you are. This kind of friendship with Jesus and the Father, through the power and wisdom of the Holy Spirit, can begin for you *today*.

7

JUST BEGIN

IN GOLF, ONE OF THE GREATEST KILLERS I SEE is when people try to play the golf swing rather than play golf. They get so wrapped up in getting the mechanics of their swing just right, trying to put all the pieces together perfectly, that they forget about simply enjoying the round. It's the same basic trap as "doing" religion: striving so hard to perform that we forget it's not about what we do for God; it's about accepting the gift of his friendship. He wants us to walk with him, enjoying the game of life, embracing the freedom found in him.

So here's one simple question: wouldn't you like to have Jesus as your best Friend too?

For a moment, take a spiritual inventory. Who is Jesus to you? Do you see him as a real person? If you have accepted his death on the cross for you and believe that God raised him from the dead, then he really is standing by your side, waiting for you to look him in the eyes so he can invite you to receive the gift of his transforming friendship. It's the one relationship that will change you, not because of anything you do or don't do, but simply because of what your Friend has already done. (And boy, do I know how hard this is to learn and receive!)

Having Jesus as your Friend is a little bit like what happens to a caterpillar on its way to becoming a butterfly. The caterpillar doesn't have to pass "caterpillaring" tests. It doesn't have to learn how to change into a butterfly. It doesn't even have to prove that it's worthy of entering the process of metamorphosis. Instead, the caterpillar transforms— changes from the inside out—simply because that process is hardwired into its very existence by its Creator.

> This is the process of transformation,
> and it has nothing to do with
> trying to change yourself.

In the same way, you can't become fully human— everything God wants you to be—because you work at it and keep all the rules and pass all the tests. It isn't about trying to change yourself, by your own effort, into what you think God wants you to be. It's about becoming a whole new person because of the companionship of the Friend walking beside you, helping you every step of the way. This is the process of transformation, and it has nothing to do with trying to change yourself.

It's much bigger than a human relationship, which can be unpredictable. It's a companionship that is never broken. You can't earn it or win it or deserve it; you can only accept it. Once you do, you can start to soar. That's what amazing grace is all about!

Nine years ago I ventured into this new journey with Jesus, building the foundation of my life on his friendship, and learning to see myself through his eyes. Believe me, there were stumbles along the way! Days when I would slink into my study, feeling the weight of guilt and shame, other days when I simply barreled through my list of things to get done, never acknowledging his ever-constant presence in my daily life. It made me realize that he is *always* loyal and committed to our relationship, even when I fail to show up.

The other major hurdle I had to overcome was my natural instinct to compartmentalize life. I know men are more prone to this fault than women, but likely we all have a tendency to put God into certain parts of our lives and not others. For many years my life was very much like a cafeteria line: vegetables in one little section of the tray, meat in another, dessert in a cup. Day-to-day living was arranged much the same way—quiet time with God in the morning, work during the day, time with family in the evening. What I've come to realize is that life is much more like a giant pot of stew. All the ingredients are mixed together and, dare I say, God is like the gravy, infusing every aspect of my life. God's presence is with me, in all the moments, in all the little details.

> There is always more to see and
> more to learn of Jesus.

It all starts with learning to see Jesus clearly. In fact, having a clear picture of Jesus is our ultimate aim. Think of the words the author of the letter to the Hebrews wrote. He spoke of "fixing our eyes on Jesus, the author and perfecter of faith" (Hebrews 12:2). We can't fix our eyes on someone if we can't see them, can we? And the more we fix our eyes on someone, the better we see them. That is the aim of a follower of Jesus—to get a better and better picture of Jesus in our minds as we build our intimate friendship with him.

This begins slowly, because we view him through the cloudy mirror of this world. Paul said, "For now we see only a reflection as in a mirror; then we shall see face to face" (1 Corinthians 13:12 NIV). Yet Christ becomes clearer and clearer to us as time goes on. We can be encouraged in this by Paul's own example. His first glimpse of Christ was through a blinding light on the Damascus Road, but years later he wrote that he was still, every day, pressing forward to get closer and closer to the prize of Christ (Philippians 3:12–14).

So you see, there is always more to see and more to learn of Jesus. I've been walking in this friendship with Jesus now for a number of years, and each day there is still so much more to learn and experience as I walk in the light of his constant friendship. What he can reveal to us about himself in our lifetime will never end, until one day we will see him face-to-face.

But first, he must become real to you. Right now, Jesus wants to become as real to you as he was to me that first morning, when I imagined him on the Disney course helping a junior golfer with his putting technique.

Now, the image of Jesus as a golfer was natural to me because golf is the world I know best. Talking to Jesus as a golfer was something I instinctively knew how to start doing because I'd been talking to other golfers my whole life.

For Cinny, a dear friend of ours, Jesus became real during a time of crisis. She reflects,

"I had always known that Jesus recognized me as his friend according to John 15:14. But it was not until my thirty-one-year-old daughter's battle and ultimate death due to cancer that I experienced in a more intimate way the depth, closeness, and comfort of Christ's friendship. Throughout her year and a half of treatment, Jesus became my companion in my car as I drove to work or the hospital, day after day. More nights than I can count, in a variety of hospitals, Jesus sat watching my daughter's painful procedures, feeling her pain as I did, and bringing a calm amidst the storm because he was there. Jesus was next to me as my family and I watched her slowly breathe her last breath and bid her farewell into his loving arms.

Jesus sat next to me on the porch each night the following year as I poured out my grief and pain for the loss of my firstborn. And he reminded me that 'Weeping may remain for a night but rejoicing comes in the morning' (Psalm 30:5 NIV). Jesus was my companion, my friend, and my comfort. What a friend I have in Jesus!"

What would it be like for you? If Jesus showed up in your world today, what would he look like? What would cause his path to intersect with yours? Picture him sitting across the table from you or next to you on the plane. What would make a conversation with him feel like the most natural thing in the world for you to experience? What would he say to you? Wouldn't you like to know what is he saying to you right now?

This is what he is offering you today.

If you desire God to touch your heart in the same way he touched mine years ago, you may wish to take the first step by finding a quiet place to sit and ask Jesus to reveal himself to you as a real person. For me, pulling up a chair and imagining Jesus sitting in it was a dynamic, practical way to meet him every day. But you don't have to start with a chair—again, there is no magic in the chair itself. The key is to situate yourself in a place that feels safe and open and to prepare yourself to receive the gift.

Next, ask Jesus to reveal himself to you as the warm, loving person he is—someone with whom you would feel comfortable having a heart-to-heart conversation. Seek the invitation he is already offering to you to know him in this intimate way. In my situation, he was a fellow golfer who loved kids. I have met others who have shared in the same experience, and to them he was a carpenter or a coach. The important thing to remember is that he desires us to engage him as a real person who is up-to-date on everything going on. Ask him to reveal himself to you in this light.

It may feel awkward at first to try this, as it was for me, and it may even feel somewhat irreverent. In no way do I want to downplay the character of our Lord Jesus, who is the King and Ruler of the universe. My heart's desire is to show him as righteous and welcoming, holy and approachable. Eugene Peterson, in his paraphrase of Hebrews 4:15, states it this way: "We don't have a priest who is out of touch with our reality. He's been through weakness and testing, experienced it all—all but the sin. So let's walk right up to him and get what he is so ready to give. Take the mercy, accept the help" (MSG). It may take some time before you begin to see him as a real person sitting next to you, but it gradually becomes easier. I also found that it became something I looked forward to every day.

Imagine sitting with Jesus every day, getting to share with him everything on your heart and experiencing his full attention on you! It still is so hard for me to believe sometimes that he likes me that much and enjoys being with me that much. He wants you to receive the same gift of his enjoyment of you too.

> Imagine sitting with Jesus every day, getting to share with him everything on your heart and experiencing his full attention on you!

Don't be misled by feelings, though, if you come away from the experience without an "emotional high." Feelings shouldn't be confused with the reality of his presence. Jesus is ready and waiting to make himself real to you. Practicing his presence is based upon Jesus' enduring promise to be with you and his promise to love you—even the person you think no one knows. Jesus sees the real you, and his love for you is beyond anything you will ever experience in this world.

One thing I've noticed as I've spent more time with Jesus is that our interactions have become more and more intimate and friend-like. He uses normal, modern-day language to talk to me. For instance, he's started calling me "Armstrong" from time to time—the same way my closest friend in real life does.

I soon discovered that the secret of this new life is simply being loyal to a friend you love. This is not some kind of hocus-pocus magic deal, but a real step into experiencing the joy of the transforming friendship of Jesus. It is the same joy the disciples experienced the first moment he walked up to them, looked into their eyes, and called them to be his friends. He is calling you to experience that same kind of friendship. And believe me, this will be one of the most powerful steps you'll ever take to knowing our wonderful Savior and Lord!

I am excited for you because so many things are going to be made clear as you take time to engage Jesus and start out each day slowly by spending time with him. As you embark upon this journey, my prayer for you, in the words of the thirteenth-century bishop St. Richard of Chichester, is that you will "know him more clearly, love him more dearly, and follow him more nearly, day by day."

> Do I love him more and allow him to
> love me more today than yesterday?

Based on this prayer, I encourage you to ask yourself three questions as you reflect on your time with Jesus each and every day:

- Do I know and see Jesus more clearly today than yesterday?
- Do I love him more and allow him to love me more today than yesterday?
- Will I walk with him more closely today than I did yesterday?

Most of all, my prayer is that you will draw close to the Father and the Son through the power of the Holy Spirit and begin to experience *life* as it was meant to be lived.

8

Practicing His Presence

I HAVE HEARD IT SAID THAT TRUE BELIEVERS ARE not people who have arrived, but those who have found the road that leads where they want to go. True believers are no longer lost, and while they aren't yet at the end of their journey, they are at the end of their wandering. The secret of this faith journey is found in seeing—through the eyes of our heart—the presence of our unseen Friend.

So how does all of this—the journey, the friendship— work in a practical way? Through the years as I have studied the Scriptures and enjoyed the presence of God, I have developed a simple way of approaching each day. While this daily practice has brought me into a deeper relationship with Jesus, it is by no means intended to be copied step by step. Each person will have their own unique way of relating to Jesus based upon their own experiences and circumstances. I merely offer this as an example of how I have been able to put into practice—and it does take practice!—daily fellowship in the presence of Jesus.

Three key guidelines have helped me in this new journey.

Meet...

Each morning starts out with time alone in the presence of God, imagining the person of Jesus right there with me. For me, this happens in my den, in my reading chair with a devotional book by Oswald Chambers, *My Utmost for His Highest*. This is a quiet, safe place for me, and the early morning hour means I can listen to my Friend and not be distracted.

I also use this time to dive into the Scriptures because they so clearly reveal who Jesus is and how he relates to his friends and to life. My favorite verses for this daily encounter are Matthew 11:28–30: "Come to Me, all who are weary and heavy-laden, and I will give you rest. Take My yoke upon you and learn from Me, for I am gentle and humble in heart; and you will find rest for your souls. For My yoke is easy and My burden is light." The picture that comes to mind here is the idea of being yoked together with him—lined up together, in the same frame of mind, willing to learn and striving toward the same goal. The Bible doesn't tell us to be yoked to Christianity or a cultural frame of mind or a moral viewpoint. It tells us to be yoked to the living God.

I have personally found that all of Scripture comes alive and is much more understandable when it is read in the light of Jesus' friendship. As you read about Jesus in the pages of the Bible, talk to him about what you notice—and feel free to ask him questions. Write down the ongoing insights you discover. And then, beyond your reading of the Bible with Jesus, as you sit and talk candidly with him about your life, continue to clarify the picture of Jesus you hold in your mind. What is he wearing? How does he gaze at you? What is it like when he smiles at you? What does his voice sound like? Record these things too.

The other important aspect of this meeting time in God's presence is learning to see myself the way God sees me. My performance-driven personality so often leaves me disgusted with myself. It becomes a tremendous battle to allow God to love me. But he offers that wonderful invitation, that gift of his love, not only in the morning, but throughout the day as he speaks to my heart, saying, "Come to me." There's no pressure anymore to feel like I have to get somewhere or achieve something in order to be okay with Jesus. He has already paid the ultimate price to bring me into fellowship with him.

> The Bible doesn't tell us to be yoked
> to Christianity or a cultural frame of
> mind or a moral viewpoint. It tells
> us to be yoked to the living God.

My quiet time, then, is used to get my heart lined up with him, under his yoke—which he has promised is easy—so that I am not beginning my day off-center and I am ready to learn from him.

How do I learn from him? By reading his Word with an open heart, knowing he is alongside of me, and engaging him in conversation. This prayer time is filled with gratitude and worship for his glory and greatness. It's not about being excited about what I want but having peace about what I am given. It is also the time when I seek his counsel on the circumstances and relationships of my life. First John 2:1 says that Jesus is our advocate, which means "one called alongside to help." How exciting to know I can begin each day with Jesus alongside me, offering his encouragement, guidance, and companionship.

Walk...

During my career, I've played hundreds of pro-am golf tournaments around the world. A pro-am team consists of one professional and three amateurs. Ironically, I've come to discover that life is really the opposite: one amateur, three professionals. We have on our team—present always—the Father, the Son, and the Holy Spirit. They are the pros, and I am the amateur. For years I had separated them—the Father in heaven, Jesus sitting at his right hand, the Holy Spirit down here—but how can they be separated if they are one God? I'm no theologian, but it seems to me that if we've been promised his presence with us here on earth, it's all of him, and God is ready to walk with us in every part of our lives. It is an "am-pro" team, and it's a team for life.

So throughout my day, I practice his presence by simply keeping Jesus in sight. It is really the process of seeing every situation through his eyes, making sure I act and react in a way that follows his lead. Whether I am wrestling with insecurities about providing for my family, or unhealthy judgments about people, or hearing those old voices and vices dragging me back into the pit, I try to make sure that I take each thought captive and hold it up to the light of Jesus. This concept is revealed in 2 Corinthians 10:5, "We are destroying speculations and every lofty thing raised up against the knowledge of God, and we are taking every thought captive to the obedience of Christ."

> It is really the process of seeing every situation through his eyes, making sure I act and react in a way that follows his lead.

The great football players know that when someone comes flying at them, they have to straight-arm the guy and keep on running. It's the same when the crud of the world comes flying at me—I straight-arm it and stay focused, always moving forward. Or, to keep the football imagery, I see temptation come flying at me like a football, and I catch it and hand it off to Jesus. When I do fall into sin, I nearly always hear Jesus saying, "Hand it to me, Wally. I died for that one…it's already covered." I've learned to receive the incredible gift of grace Jesus offered—that amazing second chance. In golf we call this the *mulligan*, a free do-over. And who doesn't like a second chance?

The image Jesus has given me is one of us standing shoulder to shoulder, facing my sin together. It's no longer me battling alone, but both of us walking as one. Remember the movie *Gladiator*? This was the unifying exclamation— "AS ONE!" It's a partnership with a warrior and a King.

My favorite Scripture to carry me through the day is found in Hebrews 12:1–2:

> Therefore since we have so great a cloud of witnesses surrounding us, let us also lay aside every encumbrance and the sin which so easily entangles us, and let us run with endurance the race that is set before us, fixing our eyes on Jesus, the author and perfecter of faith, who for the joy set before him endured the cross, despising the shame, and has sat down at the right hand of the throne of God.

Could it be that the joy set before Jesus was walking with his brothers and sisters side-by-side? I sure think so. So, while I walk with Jesus each day, I fix my eyes on him and aim to follow his lead, knowing that when I stumble, his hand of grace is always there to help me back up.

Share...

For so many years, I was caught up in the need to maintain a torrid pace of performance and achievement. Through it all, I always felt that those opportunities were platforms for becoming the best I could be, and I truly desired to use those platforms to reach people for Christ. That has always been the theme of my life. Within this frantic pace, there was still a restless, unsatisfied quest for something more. So what's different now?

What is most amazing about this newfound friendship with Jesus is the way my life has become infused with his love and presence, and how it just naturally spills over to those around me. Walking with Jesus through my day helps me respond to the needs of others in a genuine and unguarded way—no agenda, just a sincere love for people and a desire to help them on their journey. Some of the last words Jesus gave to his disciples after the resurrection were "Peace be with you! As the Father has sent me, I am sending you" (John 20:21 NIV). We have the same marching orders from our Friend and the privilege of carrying this out in his presence.

I discovered the hard way that living a life under the cloud of expectations only fires up the engines of performance. The idea of having to earn God's love, as if it were conditional, breaks the bond of pure love and friendship. Instead we need to think of the word *expectancy*, which better reflects Christ's attitude toward us. His desire is to be with us, to be a part of our lives, and for us to share his life.

> Our goal is sharing and showing love within the community where God has placed us and inviting others into the incredible friendship that Jesus offers.

Jesus also gave us a wonderful picture of what it means to live for others when he washed the disciples' feet. None of them expected that, and a few even protested! Jesus, the King of Kings, displayed a servant's heart, a willingness to get down in the dust and the dirt and show love. So our goal is this: sharing and showing love within the community where God has placed us and inviting others into the incredible friendship that Jesus offers.

My old idea of what it meant to be a sold-out believer just left me exhausted; now I see that those important disciplines—prayer, studying the Word, fasting, service—flow out of a heart in tune with God's heart. Success in those disciplines comes with knowing that I am following his lead, not pursuing my own path.

Isn't it good that the word *disciple* is embedded in the word *discipline*? What a great reminder to pattern our lives as disciples of Jesus. The New Testament shows us that Jesus' disciples were his followers and his friends, and they became the circle of men he called upon to do his work here on earth—in partnership with him. As we practice his presence as active, living disciples of Jesus, our lives become a reflection of his life.

It doesn't matter how much of a beginner you may be. It doesn't matter, either, how many holes you've got in your heart, how many failures are strewn in your wake, or how many empty accomplishments you've piled up during your laps around the performance track of Cultural Christian University. As Oswald Chambers said "there are many workers doing great things for God, but very few are walking with Jesus."

What Jesus is looking for is friends—men and women who are willing to *meet* with him, *walk* with him, and *share* the joy of that relationship with others. It takes practice, but it is an experience that will transform your life.

The best thing you can do right now is just begin.

> As we practice his presence as active,
> living disciples of Jesus, our lives
> become a reflection of his life.

Afterword

I HAVE WAITED A NUMBER OF YEARS TO WRITE THIS BOOK. I did that because I wanted to make sure the changes in my life from these daily encounters with Jesus were real. I needed to ensure that what I was learning of Jesus was consistent with the Scriptures and the testimonies of other followers who have known Jesus over the centuries.

These nine years later, I know it is real. Not only that, but I've also learned that I have not been alone in needing to learn this. Each year, I am given the privilege to share my story with hundreds of people at various speaking events, and every time I tell this story, people come up to me afterward and say, "I've never known I could relate to Jesus in such a personal way. I can see the difference between an on-again, off-again relationship with Jesus and a constant companionship with him. Thank you for helping me see how to begin!"

To give you an example, Dr. Bob Snyder, my friend and the president of International Health Services, says that his relationship with the Lord has grown as he has practiced the presence of Jesus in this way. He continues his early morning devotions as he always did, but now he sets a place for Jesus at the table with him. He places a cup of water in front of an empty chair. Then he opens his Bible and reads the Scriptures aloud with Jesus, talking to him about what he reads and asking him questions, leaving ample time to listen. As he listens, he writes down the things Jesus says to him. Bob has told me that his life has been turned upside-down through this new way of relating to Jesus.

My story has been written here so that you and many others can receive this same gift. You may be just starting out in your faith walk. Or perhaps you're somewhere down the road like I was and want to make a U-turn and start anew. Wherever you find yourself, you are invited to see Jesus, after learning my story, in your own similar yet unique way.

Over the last years, I have found that the spiritual disciplines from Dallas Willard's book that I struggled with so much have become more easily practiced and enjoyed in my life. I firmly believe that by cultivating a faith-filled imagination and spending some time each day in open, honest conversation with Jesus, you will find the same incredible gift that I found: that a daily, intimate friendship with Jesus can bring about an experience of life that is richer, more rewarding, more free of anxiety, and more joy-filled than you have ever imagined possible. Not *easier*, necessarily...but infinitely, immeasurably *better*. And you know what will happen? You will become more Christlike—and this Christlikeness will come about not because of your efforts to be like him but because you have been with him. Christlikeness is the result of Christ-closeness.

> Wherever you find yourself, you
> are invited to see Jesus in your
> own similar yet unique way.

I could fill another book with what Jesus has taught me over the years since that momentous morning in my home office. But I will leave that to be shared with you over time on our website. There, you'll find continuing insights from me for keeping Jesus in clear sight in your daily life, as well as opportunities to learn about the personal experiences others are having with Jesus and how they discovered friendship with him. (See the last page of this book for more details.)

Make no mistake—I am not an expert on this. I'm just a golfer who has learned to live in daily friendship and companionship with Jesus and who desires to make his life count for the Lord. Life is still a battle, and I certainly don't have it all together. I wish I could say that I keep Jesus on my mind every second of the day, but I don't.

The difference now, though, is that I'm not trying to change myself in my own effort. I'm not trying to please God in order to be okay. I know that I'm fully accepted, loved, and enjoyed by God, and I'm walking in companionship with Jesus through the gift of his friendship each day. I have a lot more peace and joy in my life than ever before, and I'm growing on a regular basis. This ongoing process of growth, I've learned, is the important thing. It's the real goal.

I was recently talking to a business friend of mine who had just connected with Jesus on this intimate level. He shared how his life is being changed by having realized that he is never alone and that he is walking alongside not only his Friend but the Creator of the universe—someone who knows him even better than he knows himself—each and every day. He related this to me with an analogy of what it is like for him to be in a business meeting. When he presents a business proposal with an expert by his side, he knows that his gifted partner will step in and explain any information along the way if he needs any help. Now, through his imagination, he can move into any situation with Jesus by his side, knowing Jesus will step in and direct him in a similar way whenever he has need.

This is just one example of the unlimited ways that Jesus wants to be proactively involved with our lives.

> This ongoing process of growth,
> I've learned, is the important
> thing. It's the real goal.

The other thing that I want to be very clear about is that I don't take my friendship with Jesus lightly. Even though it is an adventure and a fun daily experience, there is still a deep reverence for Jesus and his Father in my life—probably a much deeper reverence than there has ever been before!

I am deeply grateful for Jesus' love and for the opportunity to know him and his Father. My goal each day, just like my prayer for you, is to see Jesus a little more clearly today than I did yesterday. Will you join me in the daily practice of the wonderful gift of this friendship? I want so much for you to be able to say, along with me, that you know *the Friend came.*

Acknowledgments

IT WOULD TAKE ME A WHOLE BOOK to thank everyone the Lord has used to significantly impact my life and faith! But for the writing of this book, I must first thank Jesus for his patience with me for thirty-six years and for leading me to Dallas Willard, who led me to Leslie Weatherhead.

To Ander Crenshaw, who introduced me to Jesus forty-three years ago, and to my close friends Jim Hiskey, Bill Stephens, Jack Smith, and Owen Matthews for their one-on-one friendships through the years: thank you.

To Ken Blanchard, my fellow lover of Jesus, golfing buddy, and coauthor of *The Mulligan,* who provided the inspiration for finishing and publishing this book: thank you.

To Mike Mason and Father Joe Girzone: your books helped me see Jesus more clearly and have been a tremendous inspiration in my walk with Jesus. Thank you.

To those who have worked alongside me the last nine years, I thank you.

To the friends who showed Jesus more clearly to me through the years, I thank you: Jim Barker, Bill Rogers,

Todd Howard, Bill Neidlinger, Doug Coe, Kevin Harney, Dr. Bob Snyder, Don Purcell, Bob Green, Jimmy Stewart, Dr. Rick Alexander, John Smith, Jeff Armstrong, John Faulkner, Jeremy Folmsbee, Mike Regan, Shawn Munn, Joe Thiel, Richard Roles, my pastor Joel Hunter, the Tampa Bay band of brothers, and countless others. At my age, I know that I will have forgotten some friends—please forgive me any oversight.

To my wonderful wife, Debbie, and our daughter, Dana, and two sons, Scott and Blake, along with our seven grandchildren: I thank you too. Your companionship with me through this life-changing journey—as well as the laughter and memories made over the years of our life together—have been among the greatest, most treasured gifts of my life.

To the writers who have helped me in the writing of this book—Thom Lemmons, Mike Henderson, Jane Hursh, and Barb Lilland—I thank you.

Special thanks to Christianne Squires for her steadfast work as my editor on this manuscript the last few years.

Thanks to Bill Ashby for his printing help on an early version of this book, Curtis Lawrence for his development of our website, and Eli Blyden for his design work along the way.

Lastly, thank you to Summerside Press and Jason Rovenstine for the opportunity to bring this book to life.

ABOUT THE AUTHOR

DYNAMIC PROFESSIONAL GOLFER, TEACHER, AND LIFE COACH Wally Armstrong has competed in over three hundred PGA Tour events, including the British Open, the US Open, and the Masters, and was awarded a lifetime membership in the Tour. In his first Masters appearance, Wally finished in fifth place, setting a rookie record for the lowest tournament score of eight under par.

Wally attended the University of Florida and received a bachelor of science and master's degree from the College of Health and Human Performance.

As a golf instructor and clinician, Wally has taught golf all over the world and has produced more than twenty golf instructional videos and DVDs covering every area of the golf game. His teaching background and products can be viewed at www.WallyArmstrongGolf.com.

Wally is the author of seven books, including the best-selling *In His Grip* (with Jim Sheard and Billy Graham) and *The Mulligan* (with Ken Blanchard). He resides in Maitland, Florida, and has been married to his wife, Debbie, for forty-one years. Together, they have three children and seven grandchildren.

connect WITH US!

PLEASE VISIT OUR WEBSITE AT WWW.OLDPROBOOKS.COM to gain more insights about the wonderful opportunity you have to know Jesus as the real person that he is. We would love to hear from you about how you envision him and walk with him each day! It is our desire that as people share their stories on the site, we will be able to compile these stories into additional books like this one that serve as an encouragement to others, as it's really through the stories of others that we gain our greatest understanding of what it looks like to walk with Jesus.

I would love to hear from you and welcome your correspondence, either through the website, via e-mail at WallyArmstrong@OldProBooks.com, or through the mail at P.O. Box 941911, Maitland, FL 32794.

If you are interested in more information on golf products, go to www.WallyArmstrongGolf.com. To join the movement of connecting the 75 million golfers worldwide to Jesus, go to www.MulliganGolfClub.com.